Why did
THE COLD WAR
happen?

PAUL HARRISON

Gareth Stevens
Publishing

Please visit our Web site, www.garethstevens.com.
For a free color catalog of all our high-quality books,
call toll free 1-800-542-2595 or fax 1-877-542-2596.

Library of Congress Cataloging-in-Publication Data

Harrison, Paul, 1969-
Why did the Cold War happen? / Paul Harrison.
    p. cm.—(Moments in history)
Includes index.
ISBN 978-1-4339-4166-5 (library binding)
ISBN 978-1-4339-4167-2 (pbk.)
ISBN 978-1-4339-4168-9 (6-pack)
1. Cold War—Juvenile literature. 2. World politics—
1945-1989—Juvenile literature. I. Title.
D843.H315 2011
909.82'5—dc22
                    2010012456

First Edition

Published in 2011 by
Gareth Stevens Publishing
111 East 14th Street, Suite 349
New York, NY 10003

Copyright © 2011 Arcturus Publishing

Series concept: Alex Woolf
Editors: Philip de Ste. Croix and Kathy Elgin
Designer: Andrew Easton
Picture researcher: Thomas Mitchell
Project manager: Joe Harris

Photo credits: All the photographs in this book were
supplied by Getty Images, except for the cover:
Bettmann/CORBIS. The photographs appearing on
the pages listed below are Time Life images. Time Life
Pictures/Getty Images: 27, 38, 39, 40, 42, 43, 44.

Printed in the United States of America

CPSIA compliance information: Batch #AS10GS: For further information contact
Gareth Stevens, New York, New York at 1-800-542-2595.

SL001515US

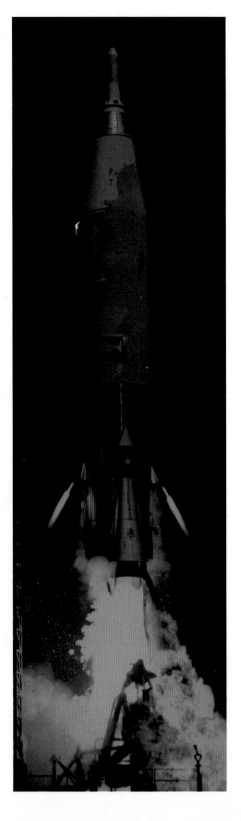

CONTENTS

CHAPTER 1

THE FREEZE BEGINS

During the 1950s, American schoolchildren could often be seen practicing a defense drill—the government's instructions about what they should do if their town was the target of a nuclear attack. The advice was to duck under a desk and roll into a ball facing away from the window. "Duck and Cover" would actually have been futile, but the possibility of attack was very real. This was during the Cold War, a conflict that lasted for nearly 50 years, transforming countries and threatening the whole planet. Our lives today were shaped by the events that unfolded during this period.

The Cold War was a global conflict between the West and the East—more specifically, the United States and the Union of Soviet Socialist Republics (USSR), or Soviet Union. These were the two major world powers, or "superpowers," as they came to be known. Since neither side actually took up arms to fight the other directly, their mutual antagonism was called a "cold" war. Each side viewed the other with intense suspicion and fear.

The start of the Cold War has sometimes been traced back as far as 1918 and the ill will generated between East and West when the U.S. and Britain sent troops to Russia to help in the fight against the newly formed Communist government. Most people, however, set the beginning of the Cold War at 1945. As World War II (1939–45)

"Duck and Cover" may have been fun to practice, but it would not have saved lives in the event of a real nuclear attack. In the 1950s, a film with this title was just one of many civil defense measures aimed at encouraging the general public to be alert to the possibility of nuclear war.

British soldiers stand by the wreckage of a train bombed by insurgents in northern Russia in 1919. Between 1918–1920, Russia was caught up in a vicious civil war in which the czarist forces, or "White Russians," fought against the Bolshevik revolutionary government, or "Red Russians." Despite American and British support for the "White Russians," the Communist forces held on to power.

ended, the Allied leaders—U.S. president Franklin D. Roosevelt, British prime minister Winston Churchill, and Soviet premier Joseph Stalin—met to discuss the final stages of the campaign and decide how the defeated Axis powers would be governed after the war.

CONFERENCE AT YALTA

In February 1945, the small Soviet town of Yalta on the Crimean peninsula was host to a crucial meeting. With war still raging in Europe and the Pacific,

VOICES FROM HISTORY

Comrades in Arms

The Western Allied leaders often found themselves disagreeing with Stalin, but he won their respect. Churchill described him as

"…this truly great man, the father of his nation."

For his part, although Stalin remained wary of the Western leaders, he could still separate personal and political feelings. After visiting an ailing Roosevelt, who suffered from polio, he said to an aide:

"Why did nature have to punish him so? Is he any worse than other people?"

Both quoted in Simon Sebag Montefiore, *Stalin: The Court of the Red Tsar* (Phoenix, 2003)

5

Hitler takes the salute as his troops occupy Poland in September 1939. Germany had made two attempts to invade Russia, just as Napoleon's French troops had a century earlier. The USSR sought to protect itself against further invasion at the conclusion of World War II.

the Allied leaders came to discuss how to defeat the Germans and Japanese, and how the world would be realigned when the war was over. The United States and Britain wanted the USSR to send troops to help fight Japan, and Stalin agreed. Next on the agenda was the formation of the United Nations (UN), an international organization of countries established to work for world peace and security. To allay the Soviet Union's fears that the other two Allies might join forces against it in the UN to promote policies that served their own purposes, it was agreed that each of the major powers would have the right of veto. The leaders also agreed

that Germany would be split into four occupied zones, with each of their countries, along with France, taking control of one section. The final issue was Poland.

The Soviet Union had been invaded through Poland twice in the space of thirty years, and Stalin wanted to safeguard against it happening again. It was decided that the Soviet border with Poland should be moved westward to extend USSR territory, while Poland would take territory from Germany. The USSR agreed that Poland could hold free elections rather than stay under Soviet control.

The Yalta Conference appeared to

TURNING POINTS IN HISTORY

How Europe was divided

The way Europe was finally divided at the Potsdam Conference was based partly on a plan that Churchill scribbled hastily on a piece of paper. When he showed it to Stalin, the Soviet leader studied the plan for a few moments and drew a big checkmark next to it to signify that he agreed.

The fate of Europe had been decided in a few short minutes. Essentially, the Soviets were to retain control of the countries their Red Army had liberated during the war, and the Western Allies would look after the rest.

This was intended to be a temporary arrangement, with elections held later to decide the fate of the occupied countries democratically. However, events were to take a very different course.

have gone well, but there were signs of deeper, underlying tensions, and these became more apparent when the Allies met again at Potsdam, near the German capital, Berlin, in July 1945. The war in Europe had ended with the Soviets entering Berlin from the east, and U.S. and British forces closing in from the west. President Roosevelt had died and been replaced by Harry Truman. Britain's Conservative Party was defeated in a general election and, during the conference, Churchill was replaced as prime minister by the Labour Party's Clement Attlee.

WAR REPARATIONS

The Potsdam Conference settled the division of Germany, but there were other areas of disagreement, namely the precise border between Russia and Poland. The other main sticking point was the payment of reparations by Germany. The United States and Britain felt that Germany should not be made to pay reparations before it was economically stable, but the USSR wanted its payments immediately. Stalin made it clear that, as over 27

The Allied leaders pose for the cameras during the Potsdam Conference in 1945. Seated in the foreground are Clement Attlee (left), Harry Truman (center) and Joseph Stalin (right). Stalin, who had considered Churchill to be an impressive leader and preferred Roosevelt to Truman, was disappointed by the change in Western leadership.

million Soviet citizens had died in the war, he was in no mood to help Germany recover. In the end it was decided that the USSR would have its reparations immediately, while the other Allies would wait. Agreement had been reached, but there was no trust between the leaders. Both East and West were wary of each other's motives, and apprehensive about the future.

The West suspected that the USSR was planning to build a Communist empire. At the end of the war, the USSR controlled a large part of Europe, including Poland, Czechoslovakia,

Hungary, Romania, Bulgaria, and Albania. It installed governments that were in broad agreement with the Soviet political system. The West's worst fears were confirmed when the free elections in Poland, promised by Stalin, voted in a Communist majority which proceeded to suppress non-Communists. By 1948, the USSR was in control of Eastern Europe. There was now a clear division between East and West. As Churchill famously described it in a speech delivered in Fulton, Missouri, in 1946, "an iron curtain has descended across the continent."

Just as alarming for the United States was the condition most of Europe was in. While the war had actually improved the U.S. economy, by 1945 Europe lay literally in ruins. This presented a twofold problem. First, the

The German city of Dresden lies in ruins after Allied bombing in 1945. Many other European cities were badly damaged during the war, and their citizens faced homelessness, disease, and starvation. This perilous situation was of grave concern to Europe and the United States.

The Marshall Plan

Although the world was now at peace, most of Europe had been devastated by the conflict. In Britain, rationing was still in force and the supply situation was getting worse. Communist militants were actively stirring up industrial unrest in France, and there was a serious threat that a disgruntled population would back them. To make matters worse, in 1947 Europe was hit by a particularly harsh winter and suffered a poor harvest. For these European nations, the Marshall Plan was a lifeline. Without its help, Europe's recovery would have taken far longer and its political future would have been more unpredictable.

A shipment of sugar arrives in Britain in 1949 as the Marshall Plan gets underway. American food and equipment were lifesavers for the impoverished citizens of many European countries. Although the USSR turned down the offer of aid, the Communist leaders of Yugoslavia did accept some American help.

United States did not want Communist influence to spread any further, but Communism is an attractive proposition to people who have nothing. Second, the economic plight of America's allies made them powerless to help in the struggle against Communism. This was particularly true of Britain, which had been funding the non-Communist side in the civil war raging in Greece but now found itself unable to continue. It was the prospect of Britain pulling out, and the probable victory of the Communist forces, that prompted the United States to implement two momentous policies.

The first of these is known as the Truman Doctrine. In 1947, Truman asked Congress for $400 million to help the anti-Communist forces in the Greek civil war. He also proposed that the United States should lend money to any country that needed help fighting Communism. Congress approved the proposal and aid was sent to the anti-Communist Greek forces and to neighboring Turkey, which was also threatened with a Communist takeover.

Truman's initial proposal was fleshed out by the Marshall Plan, an aid package named after U.S. Secretary of

9

At first it was fairly easy to move between the four different sectors into which Berlin had been divided in 1949, but as Cold War tensions increased, this became more difficult. The city's inhabitants found themselves caught up in a political standoff between East and West.

State George Marshall and designed to support the fight against Communism by offering financial aid to European countries trying to rebuild themselves. Aid would not be restricted to non-Communist countries, but would be available to Communist governments, too. The USSR, however, viewed this offer with deep suspicion and rejected the plan, which only served to drive the former allies further apart.

The Marshall Plan was not the only economic policy to cause a rift between East and West. The issue of a new German currency brought the old allies to the brink of war. At the end of World War II, Germany had been split into four zones, as had its capital city, Berlin. The United States, Britain, France, and

the USSR controlled one zone each. However, Berlin itself lay deep inside East Germany, the zone controlled by the USSR. While the United States and Britain were resolved that German recovery should be swift, this was vigorously opposed by the USSR, which feared a strong Germany.

A CITY OF TWO HALVES

In 1948, the zones controlled by the Western allies were united to form Trizonia. In the interest of speeding economic recovery, the allies announced the replacement of the reichsmark—the old German currency, now worthless—with a new deutschmark. The Soviet Union, fearing the formation of a powerful West Germany, objected, and

NATO is born

The North Atlantic Treaty Organization (NATO) was established in 1949. The founding membership consisted of eleven European countries plus the United States. The aims of NATO were to secure peace in Europe and maintain close ties between Europe and America. Lord Ismay, NATO's first secretary general, summed up NATO's purpose in this way:

"To keep the Russians out, the Americans in and the Germans down."

Lord Ismay quoted on the Peace Pledge Union web site, www.ppu.org.uk/peacematters/1999/pm_99sp_nato.html

retaliated by introducing the ostmark in East Germany, claiming this as the new German currency. The allies declared the ostmark invalid in Berlin and introduced a special version of the deutschmark, called the B-mark, to be used in the capital.

Stalin's response was to close all land links between West Germany and Berlin, effectively cutting the city off from the West. It looked as if West Berlin would be starved into submission. Some of the allies suggested breaking the blockade by force, but the United States was unwilling to risk war. Then the British

The Berlin airlift was a triumph of organization and provided the West with a means of breaking Stalin's blockade of Berlin without the use of military force. Here, crowds watch an American supply plane flying in the supplies the stranded citizens of Berlin desperately needed.

J. Robert Oppenheimer (left) was the American physicist leading the Manhattan Project. Here, he and other senior members of the team are looking at a photograph showing the explosion of the second atom bomb dropped on Japan during World War II. The bomb was detonated over the city of Nagasaki on August 9, 1945.

air force came up with a more unusual idea—flying in supplies. Nothing like this had been attempted before, and it seemed unlikely to succeed; coordination would be difficult, and the costs would be high. But the American and British governments decided to give it a try.

Bringing in supplies by air became an around-the-clock operation. At one point, a transport plane landed in Berlin every ninety seconds, and by spring 1949, 8,000 tons of supplies were arriving every day. Soviet fighter planes buzzed the transport aircraft but were unwilling to provoke an armed conflict. By May 1949, it was clear that the blockade of Berlin was not working, and on May 12, Stalin called it off. The USSR had been defeated without a shot being fired.

Throughout his dealings with Stalin,

Truman believed he had one distinct advantage—the United States had the atomic bomb, the Soviets did not. The first A-bomb, dropped on August 6, 1945, at the end of World War II, devastated the Japanese city of Hiroshima. A single bomb killed over 100,000 people, and many more became seriously ill from radiation sickness. Never before had the world seen such a powerful weapon of mass destruction.

THE MANHATTAN PROJECT

At the Potsdam Conference, President Truman told Stalin that he had a secret weapon. This was the atomic bomb, which was being developed in a top-secret program code-named the Manhattan Project. Stalin knew all too well what Truman meant: Soviet spies had been passing information about the Manhattan Project directly to Moscow.

At the time of the Berlin blockade, the United States was still the only nation to have the bomb, but in August 1949, barely three months after the blockade ended, everything changed. The USSR shocked the world by testing its first atomic bomb. The United States had known the Soviets were developing a bomb, but believed that they were years away from a successful test. Now the arms race had begun.

From then on, the United States and the Soviet Union competed to amass larger stockpiles of more powerful weapons. The hydrogen bomb—1,000 times more powerful than the atomic bomb dropped on Hiroshima—was developed in 1952. By 1957, intercontinental ballistic missiles (ICBMs) were being tested. These long-

Which side was to blame?

The arms race made the escalation of the Cold War only too visible, but historians disagree over who was responsible for provoking this increasingly serious conflict. British commentator Paul Johnson suggests that blame lies primarily with the Soviets:

"In effect Stalin had polarized the earth ... It was he who had built the Iron Curtain ... (he) hated 'Westerners' in the same way Hitler hated Jews."

Others, among them the historian Eric Hobsbawm, blame the Americans:

"Among democratic countries it was only in the USA that presidents were elected against communism ... In fact, as the rhetoric of J.F. Kennedy's electioneering demonstrates ... the issue was not the academic threat of Communist world domination, but the maintenance of a real U.S. supremacy."

Paul Johnson, *Modern Times—A History of the World from the 1920s to the 1990s* (Weidenfield & Nicholson, 1983); Eric Hobsbawm, *Age of Extremes, The Short Twentieth Century 1914–1991* (Michael Joseph, 1994)

range missiles with nuclear warheads could be launched from one continent to strike a target in another. These were followed by the development of U.S. submarines that could launch nuclear missiles from beneath the surface of the ocean.

The United States concentrated on developing better weapons, while the USSR focused on the sheer quantity of missiles it could produce. Soon, enough weapons existed to destroy all life on Earth. The superpowers were locked in a battle for supremacy that cast a shadow over the world.

ICBMs, like this one tested by the United States in 1960, changed the face of modern warfare forever because of their ability to travel vast distances. The missile in the photograph was launched using an Atlas rocket—the same as those used later to carry astronauts into space.

CHAPTER 2

THE WORLD DIVIDES

American troops go ashore at Inchon, South Korea, on September 15, 1950. The invasion was a bold gamble, but turned out to be hugely successful. The capital city, Seoul, was liberated and the North Korean army was soon driven back over the 38th parallel.

While East and West clashed over Berlin, events in Asia were taking a more dramatic course. At the end of World War II, northern Korea had been occupied by Soviet forces, while the United States took control of the south. At Potsdam, the two countries agreed to divide Korea along the latitude known as the 38th parallel, agreeing to also hold elections to unite the country. In 1949, the United States pulled its troops out of South Korea.

However, the elections never took place. In June 1950, in the absence of U.S. military forces and with Soviet approval, North Korea invaded South Korea. Northern troops rapidly occupied the southern capital, Seoul, which fell on June 28, and went on to occupy most of the country. U.S. troops, led by General Douglas MacArthur and operating as part of a combined UN force, landed in South Korea to lead a counterattack, pushing the Communist troops back over the 38th parallel. MacArthur's men continued to advance northward, capturing North Korea's capital, Pyongyang, on October 12, 1950, and forcing the North Korean troops back towards the Yalu River, Korea's border with China.

The unfortunate consequence of this was to bring China, another Communist country, into the conflict. The Chinese, unwilling to see fellow Communists suffering foreign aggression so close to their borders, sent troops to help. The Soviets, always wary of provoking war, would not commit troops, but supplied military hardware—for which, much to the disgust of the Chinese, they demanded payment. The Soviet Union and China may have been comrades in Communism, but they regarded one another with great mutual distrust. For its part, the United States had not wanted to go to war with China, but found itself with little choice. The sheer number of Chinese and Korean troops drove the UN forces back beyond the

VOICES FROM HISTORY

A forgotten conflict

Many who fought in the Korean War feel that it is "the forgotten war." U.S. veteran Ray L. Walker explains:

"As far as the American public was concerned, Korea was an unknown land of little importance ... It is also important to note that the Korean War is the first war America did not win an ultimate victory ... At the end of the war there was merely a sigh of relief in America. There were no parades, no show of national pride or support for the veterans. We just came home, and when discharged we went about building our lives"

Ray L. Walker, quoted on the Korean War National Museum Web site, www.theforgottenvictory.org

These Americans soldiers are under heavy bombardment from the North Korean army. By the end of the conflict, troops on both sides were dug into static positions.

Ethel and Julius Rosenberg, seen here on their way to prison in 1951, were convicted of spying for the USSR, and in particular of revealing atomic secrets. They were executed by electric chair in June 1953, the only Americans to be executed for espionage during the Cold War.

The dark arts

The KGB (Komitet Gosudarstvennoy Bezopasnosti, or Committee for State Security) was the Soviet Union's secret police organization, in charge of national security. It had its origins in the Russian Revolution, but the establishing of the KGB in 1954 heralded a new approach to state security.

A single organization now controlled and coordinated the running of the secret police, issuing propaganda, catching enemy spies, and dealing with any internal dissent, be it political, religious, or social. The KGB was a powerful force, a clear statement of the importance that the superpowers placed on the art of espionage.

38th parallel, and although UN troops fought back and regained lost ground, by July 1951 both sides were dug in along a line just north of the 38th parallel. It was a stalemate. Eventually, in 1953, a cease-fire was agreed to, but for three years the Cold War had heated up alarmingly.

SPY AND COUNTERSPY

The reason America had been taken by surprise by the outbreak of the Korean War was that its intelligence-gathering organization, the Central Intelligence Agency (CIA), had failed to predict it. This highlighted the importance of the role of the rival spy networks in the Cold War. As both sides spent more and more time and money trying to discover what the other side was doing, espionage became a major area

of conflict.

Planting spies in an enemy country was an effective way of gathering information, but it was also unpredictable. If an agent was captured or killed, the flow of information was lost. Training and equipping agents was also expensive and time-consuming. As the Cold War unfolded, machinery began to replace agents on the ground. Technology was becoming increasingly important.

At the forefront of this new style of intelligence-gathering was America's U-2 spy plane. This aircraft had the ability to take photographs from a very high altitude, which kept it out of the range of Soviet fighters and antiaircraft missiles.

THE USSR AFTER STALIN

In the Soviet Union, Stalin's power was absolute and he ruled with an iron fist. His vast network of spies and informers were employed not only against the West, but also to seek out opposition at home. Stalin tolerated no opposition, social or political; religion was effectively outlawed, and workers' trade unions were banned.

It was Stalin's need for total control that drove a wedge between what was then Yugoslavia and the USSR. Yugoslavia was a Communist country, but was not under the direct influence of the USSR. Stalin, however, believed that all Communist governments should obey his mandate, and when Marshal Tito, the Yugoslav leader, refused to do so, diplomatic relations with Yugoslavia were broken off.

Stalin's death in March 1953 left a power vacuum that was eventually filled by Nikita Khrushchev. It seemed

An American U-2 spy plane took this photograph of a Soviet missile site on the island of Cuba in October 1962. It provided evidence of the presence of Soviet ballistic missiles in Cuba, leading to one of the most serious Cold War confrontations between the United States and the Soviet Union.

MISSILE TRANSPORTERS

12 PROB GUIDELINE MISSILES

HEAVY EQUIPMENT

5 MISSILE DOLLIES

20' LONG CYLINDRICAL TANKS

MISSILE TRANSPORTERS

OPEN STORAGE

In the Europe of the 1950s, East and West were clearly divided, with Eastern Europe effectively sealed off by a line of Communist-controlled countries. Winston Churchill famously described this dividing line, where the NATO alliance confronted the Warsaw Pact countries, as the "Iron Curtain."

that Khrushchev's appointment as first secretary of the Soviet Communist Party might signal a new period of reform.

Khrushchev's more relaxed approach to government was tested in Poland, where strikes against wage cuts swiftly turned into a general protest against Communist control. Troops and tanks were mobilized and the protest violently put down, but Khrushchev did make some economic concessions. He also appointed Wladyslaw Gomulka to lead the government. Gomulka was not only a friend of Marshal Tito, but had also previously been imprisoned by Stalin, so his appointment felt like a move away

from the old oppressive Soviet rule.

When these events caught the attention of fellow Communists in Hungary, riots broke out in support of the Poles. Hungary wanted to leave the Warsaw Pact and become independent. Khrushchev, unwilling to allow splits to develop on his side of the Iron Curtain, sent a combination of Soviet and Hungarian troops to put down the uprising. As in Poland, a popular politician, Imre Nagy, was then appointed new leader of the Communist party.

Despite the withdrawal of troops from Hungary, the mood in the capital,

TURNING POINTS IN HISTORY

The Warsaw Pact

In 1955, worried about the power of the West's NATO alliance, most of the Eastern European Communist nations (Albania, Bulgaria, Czechoslovakia, East Germany, Hungary, Poland, Romania, and the USSR) bound themselves together by signing a treaty called the Warsaw Pact. All members were committed to giving assistance to any other member that was attacked in Europe. The Eastern Bloc was now, formally, a united military presence capable of confronting NATO head on.

Budapest, remained ugly. Workers seized public buildings, new political parties were formed, and free elections were held in some parts of the country. Nagy condoned these actions and went so far as to invite some of the new parties to form a coalition government. Finally, on November 1, he declared Hungary to be neutral and no longer under Soviet control.

For Khrushchev, this was a step too far. Thousands of Soviet troops and tanks invaded Budapest and eight days of vicious street fighting followed. Hungary appealed to the United States for help, but again the U.S. was

In a show of force, Soviet tanks patrol the streets of Budapest, Hungary, in November 1956. As the Soviet troops moved in to put down the revolution, street fighting broke out around the city, but the Hungarians stood little chance against such overwhelming odds.

The first man in space, Commander Yuri Gagarin. His mission, in April 1961, was a great propaganda victory for the USSR, and Gagarin became a national hero. By the end of the decade, however, the United States had taken the lead in the space race.

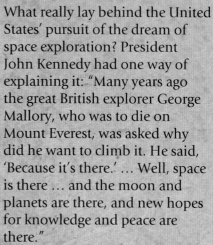

WHY DID IT HAPPEN ?

The Space Race

What really lay behind the United States' pursuit of the dream of space exploration? President John Kennedy had one way of explaining it: "Many years ago the great British explorer George Mallory, who was to die on Mount Everest, was asked why did he want to climb it. He said, 'Because it's there.' … Well, space is there … and the moon and planets are there, and new hopes for knowledge and peace are there."

But other politicians had different perspectives. President Lyndon Johnson took a tougher line: "Control of space means control of the world. From space, the masters of infinity would have the power to control the earth's weather, to cause drought and flood, to change the tides and raise the sea levels of the sea, to divert the Gulf Stream and change temperature climates to frigid."

U.S. presidents quoted in Hugh Brogan, *Kennedy* (Longman, 1996)

unwilling to confront the USSR head-on. The uprising was crushed, but not before almost 4,000 Hungarians had died and many more had fled the country. Nagy himself was arrested and executed. Hungary was not to be free.

THE SPACE RACE

The United States and the USSR may have been unwilling to confront one another militarily, but the battle for supremacy was fought out in other ways. Each of the superpowers wanted to prove to the world the superiority of its own political system. Harnessing the potential of rocket technology to launch a space vehicle was an ideal way of doing this. The USSR took an early lead in the space exploration race on October 4, 1957, when it launched the world's first satellite, *Sputnik 1*, into orbit around Earth. *Sputnik* contained a radio transmitter that sent out a beeping signal. Anyone could tune in their radios and hear it as it sped overhead.

The Soviet Union further extended its early lead on April 12, 1961, when Yuri Gagarin became the first man in space. He orbited the globe once in *Vostok 1* before returning safely to Earth. In 1961, John F. Kennedy stated that the United States would put a man on the moon before the end of the decade. It was a bold claim that not only captured people's imagination at the time but also came true.

On July 20, 1969, Neil Armstrong became the first man on the moon when he descended to the lunar surface from the landing module of *Apollo 11*. Although the rivalry continued in the 1970s and 1980s, the United States had now pulled ahead in the space race and would not look back. Funding space exploration was an expensive business which the Soviets found increasingly difficult to afford.

The second man to walk on the moon, Buzz Aldrin, followed Neil Armstrong onto the lunar surface after their historic landing on July 20, 1969. The touching down of their *Apollo 11 Eagle* landing module gave the United States a decisive lead in the space race.

CHAPTER 3

THE EDGE OF THE ABYSS

While the USSR's intervention in Poland and Hungary in 1956 met with international condemnation, the United States soon found itself the focus of widespread criticism. Involvement in an espionage scandal and the attempted overthrow of a foreign government caused the nation much public embarrassment.

Undercover activity became public news on May 1, 1960, when an American U-2 spy plane was shot down over Soviet territory and its pilot, Francis Gary Powers, was captured and imprisoned. At first, President Dwight D. Eisenhower denied the plane's existence, but Khrushchev had incriminating evidence in the form of the wrecked plane and the captured pilot.

There were more problems for the U.S. when revolution shook the island of Cuba, which lies about 93 miles (150 km) off the southeast coast of Florida. Cuba's ruler was Fulgencio Batista who, despite being a dictator, was an American ally. American businesses had invested heavily in Cuba, to the extent that most of Cuba's farmland and major companies were foreign-owned.

An armed uprising, led by leftist lawyer Fidel Castro, succeeded in overthrowing Batista's regime in December 1958 to January 1959, and Batista fled to the United States along with many other Cubans. America had lost an ally in Batista but was not openly hostile to Castro, who was not a Communist. However, the situation soon changed. In February 1960, Castro nationalized Cuba's oil and sugar industries. American companies quickly lost around a billion dollars'

Fidel Castro addresses a crowd in January 1959. In its many attempts to assassinate Castro, the CIA resorted to some highly unorthodox methods. The most famous involved a box of exploding cigars, but others focused on Castro's love of scuba diving, with plans drawn up for a poisoned wet suit and explosive-filled mollusk shells.

The failure of the Bay of Pigs invasion in April 1961 helped to strengthen the relationship between Cuba and the USSR and was a great embarrassment to the United States. Here, Cuban troops celebrate the defeat of the American-trained exiles.

worth of investments. In retaliation, the United States refused to buy Cuban sugar or to sell oil to Cuba. This trade gap was immediately plugged by Russia, bringing Castro's government and the Soviets closer together. This was a cause of great concern to the U.S.: the thought of a leftist government so close to the mainland was unacceptable.

The CIA's first response to the situation was to try to assassinate Castro, but all the attempts failed. The second plan was to arm and train Cuban exiles, believing that when the exiles returned home, the people of Cuba would rise up and join them. But the CIA was wrong. When the 1,300 exiles landed from U.S. ships at the Bay of Pigs on Cuba's southern coast in April 1961, they met with no popular support. Within three days, the hopelessly outnumbered exiles had been defeated by Cuban troops. Moreover,

TURNING POINTS IN HISTORY

Trapped in the city

The erection of the barbed wire fence around their city took Berliners by surprise. During the night of August 12–13, 1961, people found they had been separated from friends and family. Anyone who had been visiting relatives in a different sector that night found themselves trapped. Even cemeteries were split in two by the new border. The Eastern Bloc had effectively admitted that it could not compete with the attractions of the West, and the building of the wall was a clear statement of how it meant to deal with the problem—by force.

Just one of many hazardous escape attempts made in 1961 by people trying to move from East to West Berlin in the period between the city being divided and the wall being built. Some streets lay directly on the border between East and West, so that it was possible to enter a house on the Eastern side and exit the back on the Western side.

the air support promised by the United States not only proved inadequate, but was hastily withdrawn when the mission went awry and other nations began to voice their disapproval. Castro had

defeated the United States and, in the process, moved closer to the USSR.

HEAD-TO-HEAD IN BERLIN

Khrushchev followed developments in Cuba with great interest and had his eye on the performance of the new U.S. president, John F. Kennedy. Believing Kennedy too young and inexperienced for such a big job, the Soviet premier decided to put him to the test, with Berlin as the chosen venue.

Khrushchev had already made it clear that he wanted Berlin to be a neutral city free from Western control. He repeated this to Kennedy, with a veiled threat of war if his demands were not met within six months. Kennedy would not agree, though in private he questioned whether it was worth going to war over Berlin.

In a political context, Berlin was a sensitive issue. While the border between East and West Germany was heavily guarded, the border between East and West Berlin was not. People were free to move from one sector to another without undue hindrance. This was a significant issue for the East German government, as East Germans were escaping through Berlin to defect to the West. Between 1949 and 1961, around 2.6 million East Germans defected in this way, and the steady loss of so many citizens threatened the economic viability of the East German state.

But while hinting at war, Khrushchev had another plan. West Berliners woke up on Sunday, August 13, 1961, to find their city being surrounded by barbed wire. East Germany had closed the border between East and West Berlin, and for good measure ringed

The blocks that will form the Berlin Wall are laid by East German soldiers. The wall was to become a powerful symbol of West Berlin's physical isolation from the rest of the Western alliance. The German sign reads "Road closed because of the shameful wall."

25

the outside perimeter of West Berlin, sealing it off from East Germany. With both sides mobilizing tanks, war seemed inevitable. It took some frantic telephone diplomacy between Kennedy and Khrushchev to defuse the situation.

The situation was desperate for East Berliners, many of whom made frantic attempts to get to the West by jumping from buildings or trying to climb the wire. But fleeing across the border was to get even harder later in 1961, when the wire was replaced by a concrete structure complete with watchtowers and armed guards. The Berlin Wall, the most powerful physical symbol of the Cold War, had been built.

THE CUBAN MISSILE CRISIS

It was not long before the superpowers clashed again. On October 14, 1962, a U.S. spy plane photographed a Soviet missile site in Cuba. Practically all of the United States would be within range

President Kennedy speaks to the American people in a television broadcast during the Cuban Missile Crisis in 1962. The new immediacy that television brought to breaking news stories made the public feel both more involved and more vulnerable in times of crisis.

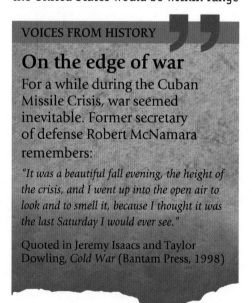

VOICES FROM HISTORY

On the edge of war

For a while during the Cuban Missile Crisis, war seemed inevitable. Former secretary of defense Robert McNamara remembers:

"It was a beautiful fall evening, the height of the crisis, and I went up into the open air to look and to smell it, because I thought it was the last Saturday I would ever see."

Quoted in Jeremy Isaacs and Taylor Dowling, *Cold War* (Bantam Press, 1998)

of missiles from this base. Khrushchev wanted to plant missiles in Cuba in retaliation for America's establishment of its own nuclear missiles in Turkey, within striking distance of most Soviet cities. Although Khrushchev made a public denial of the missiles' existence, Kennedy had the proof. He was now faced with two difficult options. He could invade Cuba, probably instigating nuclear war, or he could seek a diplomatic solution, with no guarantee of success. On October 22, Kennedy appeared on national television to explain the situation to the American people. He announced that he would be setting up a quarantine zone around Cuba, and that any Soviet ship entering the zone would be searched.

Soviet ships and a number of submarines were already on their way to Cuba when the quarantine zone was announced. Khrushchev warned Kennedy that the submarines would sink any U.S. ships that tried to stop his vessels. The situation was impossibly tense as the Soviet ships approached the edge of the zone, but at the last minute they turned back.

A U.S. destroyer escorts a Soviet cargo ship carrying missile parts away from Cuban waters. The naval blockade of Cuba almost led to nuclear war. It was a high-risk strategy on Kennedy's part, but when Khrushchev backed down, it confirmed Kennedy as a strong and decisive leader.

The United States' next move was to announce that if Soviet missiles were not removed from Cuba, it would invade the island. Soviet generals advocated launching missiles at America, but Khrushchev responded with a letter offering to remove the missiles in return for the quarantine zone being lifted and the invasion abandoned. The next day, he sent another letter demanding that if the USSR removed its missiles from Cuba, American missiles should be removed from Turkey.

Kennedy chose to ignore Khrushchev's second letter but wrote accepting the terms of the first one. At the same time, his brother Robert, the U.S. attorney general, met the Soviet ambassador.

The United States repeated its threat to invade Cuba, but suggested unofficially that it would remove the Turkish missiles. The Soviet Union agreed to Kennedy's proposals. War had been averted, but both sides realized how close they had come to nuclear war. It was a terrifying thought.

The Cuban Missile Crisis had made Khrushchev appear weak, and in 1964 he was replaced as premier of the Soviet Union. By this point the Soviet Bloc was suffering economically, crippled by the escalating cost of the Cold War. The quality of life for citizens of the East Europe Bloc was worsening steadily, and for once-prosperous countries like Czechoslovakia, such a drop in living standards was hard to bear.

THE PRAGUE SPRING

The deteriorating conditions led inevitably to civil unrest. In 1966, student protests broke out in

WHY DID IT HAPPEN

The Brezhnev Doctrine

The way in which Soviet leader Leonid Brezhnev justified sending troops into Czechoslovakia and Hungary became famous as the Brezhnev Doctrine:

"When internal and external forces, hostile to socialism, seek to reverse the development of any socialist country whatsoever in the direction of the restoration of the capitalist order, when a threat to the cause of socialism arises in that country, a threat to the security of the socialist commonwealth as a whole— this already becomes not only a problem of the people of the country concerned, but also a common problem and the concern of all socialist countries."

However, the Soviet action stunned the Czech people:

"The Soviets had said for decades they were our best friends and our brothers. They came with an army of half a million to suppress our attempt at more freedom. They came to crush it."

Leonid Brezhnev quoted in Geoffrey Roberts, *The Soviet Union in World Politics* (Routledge, 1999); Eduard Goldstucker quoted in Derrick Murphy, *The Cold War 1945–1991* (Collins Educational, 2003)

Czech students demonstrate in Prague in support of Alexander Dubček following the Soviet invasion of Czechoslovakia in August 1968. Student demonstrations were a common feature of civilian unrest in the Soviet Bloc during the Cold War years.

Czechoslovakia, and discontent simmered until 1968, when the Soviets installed Alexander Dubček as head of the Czech Communist Party. It was hoped that Dubček, a popular and sympathetic politician, might calm the situation.

Dubček was sympathetic to the calls for change and pushed through a number of political reforms. Some press restrictions were lifted, allowing people to criticize the government for the first time. Government loosened its grip on business, and trade unions were permitted to negotiate with employers. Czechs were allowed to travel abroad more freely. This blossoming of freedom in the Czech capital earned this period the nickname "the Prague Spring."

In Moscow, however, this policy of liberalization was not well received. The new Soviet leadership under Leonid Brezhnev was apprehensive about where it might lead, and would not tolerate any threat to the Warsaw Pact. If these political changes were permitted in Czechoslovakia, other members of the

Czechs look on as Soviet tanks patrol the streets of Prague in August 1968. The Soviet Union used such blatant shows of force as an effective tactic to keep unruly Communist countries in line.

Warsaw Pact might seek to make similar changes. Soviet tanks were dispatched to the Czech border.

In fact, Dubček was a loyal Communist and had no plans to leave the Pact. However, when he invited the Yugoslav leader, Marshal Tito, to Prague, the Soviets became even more alarmed. It seemed as if Czechoslovakia might try to follow Yugoslavia's lead and become independent. On August 20, Soviet forces crossed the Czech border and headed for Prague. The Czech government offered no resistance to the invasion. This prevented a repeat of the Hungarian bloodshed. Dubček was taken to Moscow and made to renounce the reforms he had overseen. He was replaced as leader by a more Soviet-friendly politician, Gustav Husák. The message to Czechoslovakia and the rest of the Warsaw Pact was clear. Any change would be met with force.

CHAPTER 4

DISTANT CONFLICTS

As the countries of the Eastern Bloc struggled to free themselves from Soviet oppression, America was facing problems of its own in Southeast Asia. For a long time, Vietnam had been part of the French colonial empire. After World War II, the Vietnamese, under their Communist leader Ho Chi Minh, fought for independence from French rule. When the French withdrew in 1954, Vietnam was split in two. North Vietnam was controlled by the Communists under Ho Chi Minh; South Vietnam was ruled by the unpopular, but U.S.-backed, Ngo Dinh Diem.

Included in the ceasefire agreement was a provision for elections to be held in 1956 to reunite the country. Diem ignored the deadline, so North Vietnam resolved to reunify the country by force. In 1959, Communists already in South Vietnam were organized into a force known as the Vietcong, with the aim of overthrowing the Diem government. The Vietcong were both advised and supplied by North Vietnam.

Diem's rule was problematic for the United States. However, the United States was saved from direct intervention when a group of powerful South Vietnamese generals rebelled and assassinated Diem in a coup in November 1963. The generals maintained the fight against the Vietcong, and the country continued to receive U.S. military aid.

In private, President Kennedy

This photograph of Ho Chi Minh was taken in 1945 when he was fighting for Vietnamese independence from the French. "Uncle Ho," as he was known, died in 1969 while Vietnam was still embroiled in a ferocious war against the United States.

believed that the South could not hope to win the fight against Communism. But just three weeks after Diem's death, Kennedy was also assassinated. The new president, Lyndon Johnson, was determined not to lose Vietnam, even if this meant all-out war with the North.

ESCALATION

In 1964, North Vietnamese troops were already marching south to help the Vietcong when the United States claimed that its warships had been attacked by North Vietnamese torpedo boats in the Gulf of Tonkin. On August 7, 1964, Congress passed the Gulf of

How it began

America's involvement in Vietnam stemmed from a fear that if Vietnam fell to the forces of Communism, the destabilizing effect on surrounding Asian countries might cause them also to topple to communism in quick succession. This was known as the domino effect. The United States was so concerned by this threat that it was willing to commit its own troops to support the South Vietnamese regime. This is why in 1965, America was drawn into the biggest armed conflict it had experienced since World War II.

Tonkin Resolution, giving the U.S. president free reign to repel attacks on U.S. forces by any means. The United States started bombing North Vietnam and sent troops to the south to join the fight. By July 1965, more than 180,000 U.S. troops had arrived in Vietnam. By 1968, this figure had risen to 540,000.

The U.S. troops would probably have proved more than a match for any other army in open conflict, but the Communists did not intend to fight an open war. Instead they used the guerrilla tactics of concealment, sabotage, and lightning fast attacks, followed by a swift retreat into the dense jungle. The U.S. forces relied on technology to counter these tactics. They dropped defoliants on forest areas to strip away the vegetation that provided the Vietcong with hiding places, and bombed supply lines and

Vietcong guerrillas on patrol during the Vietnam War. The Communist fighters proved more than a match for U.S. troops, employing the tactics of concealment, ambush, and their knowledge of the landscape to overcome their enemy's technical superiority.

The Boeing B-52 Stratofortress bomber was one of America's most powerful weapons. Able to carry around 70,000 pounds (31,750 kg) of bombs, the B-52s were responsible for devastating large areas of North Vietnam. However, these strikes were of limited effectiveness against the elusive and determined Communist forces.

towns. More bombs were dropped on Vietnam than on Germany during World War II. But the bombing campaign merely served to anger and kill Vietnamese civilians, and strengthened the resolve of the North Vietnamese.

In January and February of 1968, a strategic Northern attack on important towns in the south, known as the Tet Offensive, carried the fighting to the grounds of the American embassy in the southern capital, Saigon. The Tet Offensive failed to bring down the south, but it did have a major effect on the United States, where the government now had to confront the

possibility that the war might not be won. There was pressure, too, from public opinion at home. This was the first war to be covered day-to-day by the media: seeing that the campaign was going badly, U.S. voters began to turn against the war. On March 16, 1968, these feelings were strengthened by news reports that U.S. troops had massacred more than 300 Vietnamese civilians in the village of My Lai.

In November 1968, the U.S. elected a new president, Richard Nixon, who began looking for a way to get the U.S. out of the war. However, peace talks went slowly, and it was not until

1973 that the United States was finally able to withdraw, leaving the defense of the south in the hands of South Vietnamese forces. Two years later, the north invaded the south, and without U.S. support the country was quickly overrun. Vietnam had cost America billions of dollars in aid and more than 55,000 American lives. However, in the end, all of this sacrifice had not been enough to prevent the country from becoming Communist.

COMMUNIST CHINA

China had been Communist since 1949 when, after a long civil war, the forces of the Communist leader Mao Zedong

VOICES FROM HISTORY

Public attitudes about Vietnam

It has been argued that it was a major change in the public perception of the Vietnam War in America that caused it to end as it did. A journalist describes a peace march of 300,000 people in 1971:

"Never before in this country have young soldiers marched in protest against the war in which they themselves have fought and which is still going on."

John Pilger, quoted in Tony McAleavy, *Superpower Rivalry* (Cambridge University Press, 1998)

A member of the U.S. 1st Air Cavalry division signals to a helicopter about to land in a field north of Saigon. Helicopters were invaluable for ferrying troops and supplies quickly from place to place over the inhospitable Vietnamese countryside.

33

defeated the Nationalist forces of Chiang Kai-shek. The United States had supported the Chinese Nationalists with aid, but it was not enough to stop Mao. The Communists took control of the country.

There was disagreement between China and the USSR over a number of issues, and fundamental to these arguments was the principle of Chinese autonomy. China was opposed to the USSR's treatment of Hungary and Czechoslovakia and was not prepared to be just another satellite state agreeing to every Soviet decree. The Soviets, however, wanted the West to be presented with a unified Communist front. Such differing attitudes made conflict inevitable.

Communist troops take prisoners of war outside Shanghai in May 1949. The Chinese civil war lasted from 1927 to the end of 1949, when the Communist forces under Mao Zedong eventually defeated the Nationalists and took control of the country.

CHINA TAKES ITS OWN PATH

In 1958, China attacked islands off Taiwan, the last stronghold of Chiang Kai-shek and the Chinese Nationalists, without first telling the USSR. The Chinese action nearly brought the U.S. into a war to defend its old ally, so it was a definite matter of concern to the Soviets. Conflict with the U.S. did not bother the Chinese, who had already fought against U.S. forces in Korea. China thought the USSR had gone soft, while the USSR considered China too extreme. When the Soviets withdrew their advisers from China's nuclear bomb program, China went ahead and built the bomb without Soviet help, testing it on October 16, 1964.

In 1969, disagreement about policy finally turned into military action. Old territorial conflicts over the Russo-China border that dated back to the late 1800s escalated into skirmishes and military engagement. The two big Communist neighbors were clearly not seeing eye-to-eye. This schism was skillfully handled by President Nixon,

The SALT treaties

The SALT 1 treaty did help to limit the numbers of ICBMs that the United States and the USSR could deploy in their defense. However, as many other types of missiles were not covered by the treaty, the overall effect of the SALT agreement was limited. Nevertheless, the very fact that the rival superpowers were prepared to sit down and talk to one another was a real turning point in the Cold War. A SALT 2 treaty was signed in 1979, but it was not formally ratified by the U.S. Senate when the USSR invaded Afghanistan.

President Nixon visits the Great Wall of China with his wife Pat (right) in 1972. Although the presidential visit achieved little in real terms, photo opportunities such as this provided great publicity for Nixon's history-making diplomatic mission.

who employed some accomplished diplomacy to diffuse tension and bridge the divide. In February 1972, he became the first U.S. president to visit China. Although the meeting itself actually achieved very little, the mere fact that Nixon had deemed it necessary to visit China confirmed that country's status as a new superpower.

The thought of China and the U.S. as friends was of serious concern to the USSR's leaders. They were now eager to meet with Nixon themselves, and in May 1972, he became the first U.S. president to visit Moscow. This time, the business concluded was significant, with the Soviet Union and the U.S. signing the first Strategic Arms Limitation Treaty (SALT 1), which slowed the pace of the arms race. The two superpowers also reestablished trade links and a new era of peaceful coexistence seemed to be on the horizon. This period, when the strain on international relations eased, is often referred to as the détente.

However, the détente was to be short-lived. The USSR and the United States found a new reason to disagree with one another, and this was Afghanistan. In 1978, the new pro-Soviet government led by Nur Taraki signed a treaty of friendship and cooperation with the USSR. When Taraki's government proved to be unpopular with Afghanistan's more radical Islamic groups, civil war soon broke out.

The war was a problem for the USSR, as it threatened the loss of a Communist partner. The Afghan government was asking for help, but the Soviets were reluctant to get involved in an armed conflict. The United States, however, was supplying and training the Islamic rebels, called the mujahideen.

35

The United States invested a good deal of time and money in training the Afghan rebels to fight the Soviet invaders. Mujahideen fighters are photographed here posing proudly next to a downed Soviet helicopter in 1979.

INVADING AFGHANISTAN

In December 1979, U.S. spy satellites revealed that Soviet troops were gathering on the Afghan border, prompting U.S. president Jimmy Carter to ask Brezhnev if the USSR was preparing to invade. Brezhnev denied this, but the very next day Soviet troops went into Afghanistan. Brezhnev claimed that they had been invited, but to most of the world it appeared that this was a Soviet invasion. A furious Carter cut trade links with the USSR. Détente was over.

This intervention was a disaster for the USSR, comparable in many ways with the U.S. experience in Vietnam.

The mujahideen fought a guerrilla war, using Afghanistan's mountainous terrain to their advantage. Although Soviet troops controlled the large population centers and the capital, Kabul, the rebels held much of the countryside.

A more unexpected but nonetheless high-profile casualty of the Afghan conflict was the 1980 Olympic Games. These were due to be held in Moscow. However, Carter announced that the United States would boycott the games and urged other countries to do the same. While most nations ignored his call, the competition was compromised by the absence of the American teams,

The USSR revises its position

The USSR had at first been reluctant to respond to the Afghan leader Nur Taraki's request for Soviet aid, although he was a fellow Communist. It feared the West's response:

"The negative factors (of sending troops to Afghanistan) would be enormous. Most countries would immediately go against us."

By the end of 1979, though, the position had changed. It looked increasingly likely that the Soviet Union might lose an ally and leave itself exposed:

"In this extremely difficult situation, which has threatened … the interests of our national security, it has become necessary to render additional military assistance to Afghanistan."

The USSR had committed itself to fighting a war that many Soviets rightly believed it ultimately could not win.

Aleksei Kosygin, quoted in Jeremy Isaacs and Taylor Dowling, *Cold War* (Bantam Press, 1998); report on events in Afghanistan by Yuri Andropov, Andrei Gromyko, and others quoted on www. hartford-hwp.com/archives/51/337. html.

which included some of the world's best athletes. Now, with relations between the superpowers at a low point, the Cold War was about to get even colder.

As the Americans had discovered in Vietnam, small groups of committed men fighting in difficult terrain can triumph over more sophisticated armies. Lightly armed Afghan guerrillas like these were highly effective against the better-equipped Soviet invaders.

CHAPTER 5

COMING IN FROM THE COLD

By 1981, the American economy was booming, riding high on the rising wave of new technologies. By contrast, the USSR was still largely an agricultural nation, with an unproductive economy that was being crippled by the financial burden of the Cold War. The USSR was having difficulty trying to keep up with American advances in the spheres of finance, technology, and the military.

When Ronald Reagan replaced Jimmy Carter as U.S. president, his plan to gain further advantage over the USSR was quite simple —the United States would increase its defense budget. America would spend its way to victory

This sleek aircraft is the Rockwell B-1B long-range strategic bomber. It was just one of many new weapons developed in the 1980s by the United States.

Star Wars

The Strategic Defense Initiative (SDI) had the potential to change the shape of warfare entirely, making it a crucial turning point in the history of the Cold War. The development of ICBMs had meant that one country could make a long-distance attack on another without a soldier or pilot ever leaving base. With SDI, space itself would become the theater of war. It was not only the Soviet Bloc that was disturbed by Reagan's plans. Many in the West, too, were uneasy about the prospect of this ever-widening area of military activity. Antinuclear protest movements were now joined by people voicing their concerns about taking the arms race into space.

A space-based interceptor vehicle heads toward impact with a nuclear warhead aimed at the U.S. in this artist's impression of the Star Wars program. Many were relieved that Reagan's dream of intercepting nuclear missiles in space stayed on the drawing board.

over Communism, with the knowledge that the USSR had no hope of matching its expenditure. Reagan immediately increased the budget by over $30 billion and ordered new nuclear submarines and bombers. U.S. nuclear missile bases were established in Britain and Germany. Support was also given to anti-Communist rebels in Nicaragua and to the right-wing military dictatorship of El Salvador, engaged in a battle against left-wing guerrillas.

On the face of it, there seemed little point in increasing spending on new

nuclear weapons when each side already had enough warheads to guarantee the destruction of any country involved in an all-out war. However, Reagan had a new and startling plan. The Strategic Defense Initiative (SDI) proposed the development of satellites and ground-based systems that could shoot down incoming Soviet missiles before they hit their targets. This futuristic approach to defense was nicknamed Star Wars.

This strategy alarmed the Soviet leaders, who realized that if SDI were to succeed, the balance of power in the Cold War would swing firmly in the U.S.'s favor. In 1983, tensions increased when NATO troops took part in large-scale maneuvers. Suspecting that these were a cover for a real nuclear attack, the USSR immediately put its forces on standby. Not since the Cuban Missile

Mikhail Gorbachev (right) is shown the New York skyline by Vice President George Bush (left) and President Ronald Reagan (center) in 1988. The mutual respect established between Gorbachev and Reagan was a significant factor in bringing the Cold War to an end.

Crisis of 1963 had nuclear war seemed so likely.

The USSR's readiness to retaliate worried Reagan. He, too, realized that war had been a possibility. The stakes had been raised militarily, socially, and politically, and tensions were increasing. There were frequent antinuclear weapons protests in Europe, and, in another indication of the fragility of East-West relations, the Soviets boycotted the 1984 Olympic Games in Los Angeles. Obviously, things had to change, and when Mikhail Gorbachev became the new Soviet premier in 1985, change was definitely on the horizon.

GORBACHEV THE REFORMER

Mikhail Gorbachev was a reformer only too aware of the perilous state the USSR was in. With the ballooning defense expenditure draining the economy, and corruption rife throughout the Communist Party system, the standard of living for ordinary Russians was dire. Gorbachev began by implementing a policy of perestroika, or restructuring. One of the first measures was to ease the hold that central government had on industry, in the hope of spurring initiative and making the country more productive. However, the economy had been so neglected and was so unproductive that little progress was

The race is over

When Mikhail Gorbachev met President Reagan for talks in Geneva in 1985, it was because he realized that the only way to give the Soviet economy a chance of recovery was to bring an end to the arms race. But it was not until 1987 that a landmark agreement was reached. All nuclear missiles would be removed from Europe, and the number of ICBM missiles deployed was to be reduced, rather than simply agreeing on upper limits. The arms race was effectively over.

made. This left Gorbachev open to criticism from all sides.

Gorbachev found himself trapped between the old-fashioned Soviet Communists who disapproved of his reforms and a younger generation who wanted to see even more of them. Defense expenditure had to be cut to boost the economy, and this could only be achieved by scaling down military operations. In the hope of reducing the number of missiles it needed to keep in operation, the USSR entered into new arms talks with the United States, and in 1988, Gorbachev decided to pull Soviet troops out of Afghanistan, ending Soviet involvement in that country the following year.

In a speech to the United Nations later that year, Gorbachev announced a

The USSR prepares to pull its tanks and troops out of Afghanistan in 1989. The invasion of Afghanistan and other ill-advised military operations had cost the USSR vast sums of money. With the economy in decline, this was money it could not afford to spend.

Glasnost

Mikhail Gorbachev's second attempt at reform was glasnost, or openness. The press was given more freedom, criticism of the government was tolerated, and previously banned books could be read. Glasnost was the catalyst for change.

"Without glasnost there is not, and there cannot be, democratisation, the political creativity of the masses and their participation in management."

Mikhail Gorbachev quoted on the Web site www.nationalcoldwarexhibition.org.

These were the extraordinary scenes in Beijing's Tiananmen Square in May 1989 as protestors gathered for a pro-democracy demonstration. The demonstration was ruthlessly crushed by the Chinese government.

reduction of hundreds of thousands of personnel in the Soviet army. Over the next few months it also became clear that, in a break from the principles of the Brezhnev Doctrine, Soviet forces would no longer necessarily be sent to support other Communist governments, or Soviet troops sent to quell uprisings in the Eastern bloc.

The reforms Gorbachev implemented were the catalyst for a series of remarkable upheavals across most of the Communist world. In January 1989, the Hungarian government sanctioned the establishment of new political parties and scheduled elections for the following year. As the last Soviet troops pulled out of Afghanistan in February, Soviet troops in Hungary were preparing to do the same the following month. In May, Hungary opened its border with Austria, cutting down the barbed-wire fences that had long separated the two countries. Many Eastern Europeans seized the opportunity to flee to the West through Hungary's open border.

WINDS OF CHANGE

The breath of fresh air blowing through the Communist world reached as far as China. Gorbachev's visit to Beijing in May 1989 coincided with massive pro-democracy demonstrations. Huge numbers of protesters, most of them students, gathered in Tiananmen Square. On June 3–4, after Gorbachev had left, Chinese troops moved in and crushed the protest, killing more than 1,000 of the demonstrators. All this happened in full view of the world's media.

Meanwhile, in Poland, a happier story was unfolding. For many years, the country had been plagued by serious industrial unrest. Striking workers had formed an organization called Solidarity to coordinate trade union activity and, under the inspired leadership of Lech Walesa, Solidarity had become so popular that the Polish government had had to resort to martial law to restore its own power. Now, after months of talks between the government and Solidarity, free elections were to be held. Solidarity performed exceptionally well in the polls, and by August a non-Communist government, of which Solidarity members formed a major part, was in power.

The sense that the old order was passing away in Eastern Europe grew stronger by the day. In October 1989, people in East Berlin took to the streets demanding change. As the demonstrations grew in size, Gorbachev suggested to the East German government that the wall surrounding West Berlin should come down, and on November 10, the border was hastily opened. East Germans streamed through in celebration, some bringing hammers and chisels to attack the wall.

Celebrating Germans take over the infamous Berlin Wall in November 1989 in emotional scenes that would have been unthinkable just a few months before. The opening of the border between East and West Berlin finally reunited friends and families after nearly thirty years of separation.

Germans celebrate reunification in October 1990. Economic problems followed, however, as West Germany sought to raise the living standard of those from the East. After the initial euphoria, many experienced "ostalgie;" nostalgia for the certainties of the old life in the East.

WHY DID IT HAPPEN

The Cold War legacy

Is the legacy of the Cold War greater safety? Has the fear that embraced school pupils and presidents alike gone away? Here is one view: "The world is far safer for the Cold War's ending … It is hard now to realize or recall it, but whole generations in our time lived with the fear that one crisis or another … might trigger a nuclear holocaust."

Of course, not everyone agrees. Many commentators believe that there is a new and serious nuclear threat from terrorist organizations seeking to obtain nuclear material from former Soviet states. President Obama has said that "The single biggest threat to U.S. security, both short-term, medium-term, and long-term, would be the possibility of a terrorist organization obtaining a nuclear weapon."

Jeremy Isaacs and Taylor Dowling, *Cold War* (Bantam Press, 1998); Barack Obama quoted on http://news.bbc.co.uk/1/hi/8614695.stm

By the end of the year, Czechoslovakia's Communist government had fallen in a peaceful revolution, and in December, Romania also saw regime change. A bloody uprising led to the overthrow and execution of its Communist dictator Nicolae Ceausescu, and his wife. The Iron Curtain had finally been torn down.

In the autumn of 1990, the USSR—along with the United States, Britain, and France—agreed to the reunification of Germany. Many see this as the point at which the Cold War ended. Fear of a strong unified Germany had been a major cause of the split between the USSR and its former allies at the start of the Cold War. Now it was the issue that ended it. To allay Soviet fears, the United States assured President Gorbachev that Germany's military operations would come under the banner of NATO.

Many of the Soviet republics looked enviously at the new freedoms being enjoyed by their former Communist partners. In one year, the republics of Lithuania, Estonia, Kazakhstan, Latvia, Ukraine, Armenia, Turkmenistan, Tajikistan, and Kyrgyzstan all either declared, or voted for, independence. In an attempt to prevent the USSR from breaking up like this, Gorbachev tried a mixture of force and reform.

In November 1990, he proposed a new treaty that would bind the Soviet republics together more loosely than before, but when unrest broke out in Lithuania and Latvia, Russian troops were deployed and civilians killed. Gorbachev's attempts to appease both modernizers and the old guard with a mixture of reform and tough military action only succeeded in losing friends and gaining enemies. Although the majority of the republics voted in the proposal for the new union, some boycotted the vote, and this move was supported by Boris Yeltsin, the influential leader of the largest of the republics, Russia. Gorbachev was losing his grip.

In August 1991, old-guard Communists staged a coup and put Gorbachev under house arrest. But people had had a taste of freedom, and a return to the old days held no attraction for most Russians. Without the support of the public and, crucially, the army, the coup failed. Gorbachev was freed, but the balance of power had shifted towards Yeltsin. Gorbachev resigned. The new union treaty was never implemented. Instead, a new Commonwealth of Independent States (CIS) was formed, an idea championed by Yeltsin. All the former members of the USSR—except the Baltic states of Estonia, Latvia, and Lithuania—joined the CIS. By the end of 1991, both the Cold War and the USSR had been consigned to history.

The political world map of 2010 was very different from that of 1955 (see page 18). Europe was no longer fundamentally divided between East and West, and there were far fewer Communist-controlled states.

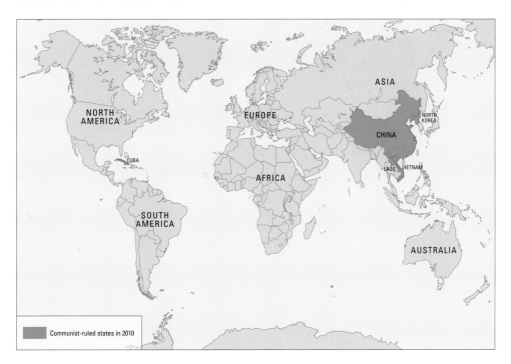

Communist-ruled states in 2010

COLD WAR TIMELINE

1945

February 4–11: Yalta Conference

July 17–August 2: Potsdam Conference

August 14: End of World War II as the Japanese accept terms of surrender

1948

June 24: Berlin blockade begins

1949

April 4: NATO alliance formed

May 12: End of Berlin blockade

October 1: Communist forces under Mao Zedong take control of China

1950

June 25: Korean War starts

1953

July 27: Korean War ends

1955

May 14: Warsaw Pact formed

1957

October 4: *Sputnik 1* launched by Soviet Union

1960

May 1: American U-2 spy plane shot down over Soviet territory

1961

April 17: Bay of Pigs invasion of Cuba

August 13: Berlin divided

1962

October 16–28: Cuban Missile Crisis

1965

March: President Johnson orders U.S. troops into Vietnam

1969

July 20: First moon landing made by *Apollo 11* crew

1972

May 26: SALT 1 arms limitation treaty signed by United States and USSR

1973

January 27: Vietnam War ends

1979

December 25: Soviet forces invade Afghanistan

1983

March 23: Ronald Reagan announces Strategic Defense Initiative

1985

March 11: Mikhail Gorbachev takes power in the USSR

1987

December: Reagan and Gorbachev sign Intermediate Nuclear Forces Treaty

1989

January: Soviet troops withdraw from Afghanistan

June 3–4: Chinese troops crush pro-democracy protest in Tiananmen Square

August: Non-Communist government elected in Poland

September: Hungary becomes independent

November 10: Berlin Wall falls

November 17–27: Nonviolent revolution in Czechoslovakia

December 21: Revolution in Romania

1990

October 3: East and West Germany reunite

1991

July: Warsaw Pact officially dissolved

December 8: Commonwealth of Independent States formed as successor to the USSR

Glossary

atomic bomb A very powerful bomb in which an explosion is caused by nuclear fission, splitting the nuclei of atoms.

autonomy The right of a country to govern itself.

bloc A group of united countries.

blockade The act of surrounding a place to prevent exit from or entry into it.

coalition A group of people, governments, or countries united on a temporary basis.

Communism A political system based on state control of the economy and people sharing wealth and property.

coup The overthrow of a government.

defect To change sides, or leave one country for another.

defoliants Weapons designed to kill vegetation.

democracy A form of government freely elected by the people.

espionage Spying.

guerrillas Small groups of irregular soldiers usually fighting against a much larger organized army.

insurrection An uprising.

intercontinental ballistic missile (ICBM) Rocket-based weapon which can strike another country thousands of miles away.

Islamic From Islam, the world religion revering one god, Allah, and his prophet, Muhammad.

liberalization The process of becoming less hard-line and more open to change.

militants Aggressive, hard-line supporters of a particular religious or political cause.

propaganda Printed or broadcast information that tries to persuade people that a particular cause is good or bad.

quarantine zone An area where movement in or out is restricted.

rationing The act of restricting the amount of vital supplies, such as food or fuel, that a population can receive.

reparations Money paid by a defeated country to the victors to pay for damages sustained during a war.

Further Information

Books:

Blohm, Craig E. *An Uneasy Peace, 1945–1980.* San Diego, CA: Lucent, 2003.

Bjornlund, Britta. *The Cold War.* San Diego, CA: Lucent, 2002.

Brager, Bruce L. *The Iron Curtain: The Cold War in Europe.* Broomall, PA: Chelsea House, 2004.

McNeese, Tim. *The Space Race.* New York: Children's Press, 2003.

Stein, R. Conrad. *The Cold War.* Berkeley Heights, NJ: Enslow, 2002.

Web Sites:

About CIA (www.cia.gov/about-cia/index.html)

Cold War (www.globalsecurity.org/military/ops/cold_war.htm)

The Cold War Museum (www.coldwar.org)

President Truman and the Origins of the Cold War (www.bbc.co.uk/history/worldwars/wwtwo/truman_01.shtml)

INDEX

Numbers in **bold** refer to pictures